I Am You

ANNE TARDOS is a poet and visual artist. She is the author of several books of poetry and the multimedia performance work and radio play *Among Men*. A selection of her readings and performances (many with Jackson Mac Low) can be heard on the University of Pennsylvania's web site PennSound: http://writing.upenn.edu/pennsound/x/Tardos.html and her own site is www.annetardos.com

Also by Anne Tardos

I Am You

ANNE TARDOS

SALT

CAMBRIDGE

PUBLISHED BY SALT PUBLISHING
PO Box 937, Great Wilbraham, Cambridge CB21 5JX United Kingdom

First published 2008

Printed and bound in the United Kingdom by Biddles Ltd, Kings Lynn, Norfolk

Typeset in Swift 9.5 / 13

ISBN 978 1 84471 442 1 paperback

Salt Publishing Ltd gratefully acknowledges
the financial assistance of Arts Council England

1 3 5 7 9 8 6 4 2

To Jackson Mac Low

Contents

Acknowledgements

Michael Byron's support and encouragement were key. I thank him. And I thank Bradford Morrow, editor of *Conjunctions* #48, for publishing "The Aim of All Nature Is Beauty"; Tracy Grinnell, editor of *Aufgabe* #5, for publishing "The Nature of this Lecture Is by John Beauty"; and Marie Buck and Brad Flis, editors of *Model Homes* #1, for publishing excerpts from "Letting Go."

Special thanks to Susan Wheeler for her uncomplicated and powerful support, and thanks to Christina Strong for her openness to new ideas. John Kinsella's eye for poetry and Chris Hamilton-Emery's hand in turning the book into reality are to be thanked and admired.

Introduction

I've always found Anne Tardos's work thrilling. While there is much to be fascinated with, Tardos's treatment of poetry's 'I,' both here and in her earlier volumes, is strange, transformative, completely unnerving. The neologisms and non-normative syntax of Tardos's *Uxudo* and *The Dik-dik's Solitude* ask me to read without referring to a lyric 'I'—without allowing me to identify with an author-figure or a character. While *I Am You* retains some neologistic and asyntactic elements, it also introduces meditative and talky speaking subjects that haven't appeared in Tardos's earlier work. Through these speakers, *I Am You* both forefronts subjectivity and picks it apart. As elegy, this book must necessarily take up the question of autobiography. And in taking up autobiography, Tardos uses commonplace phrases and a flagging of form's contortions to move through and rupture those ideas associated with autobiography: that a person's life follows a linear narrative, that a person is in fact the same person from one moment or year to the next, that one must "let go" of people and the past throughout one's life. "It should really be called 'selves.' There are so many of us assembled/here," writes Tardos, and *I Am You* really does feel like an elegy written by a plurality of subjects.

One of the fixations in the poem "Letting Go" is monstrosity. If one is not really the same person from one moment to the next, there is indeed something monstrous about the forcing of self into the particular rigid forms allowed by language. If the narratives by which an 'I' changes are unfamiliar (or defamiliarized), what might be described in some contexts as 'evolution' or 'progress,' instead appears as monstrosity or distortion. So the 'I' becomes monstrous in the tension of its having the appearance of a stable, specific subject, and always being in a state of change. One can never fit exactly, must always be figured as outside of the bounds of what's considered 'human.' A monster, just like the monster of any horror movie: the changing self in a rage as it realizes its own 'disfigurement,' its inability to fit into grammatical forms of self and thus its status as cast out from everyday discourse.

I Am You is chatty and colloquial, frequently reiterating and altering bits of thought and conversation. In correspondence about her work, Tardos wrote that these poems are "pop," and these poems' attention to popular language brings up questions: how does a reader account for the monstrosity of language, the misfitting 'I' in her everyday speech? How do you acknowledge the shifting nature of your self in the loaded and worn-out language you're limited to in describing grief, morphing, alteration? Once you recognize the monstrosity of using a single, static letter 'I' to stand in for such a diversity of versions of yourself, what might you say? *I Am You* gives you characters able to critique the notion of character, pop phrases used to explain what's reductive about pop phrases, elegy attacking elegiac conventions so that this elegy might be written.

"The Aim of All Nature Is Beauty" contains images of Colette and her dog Toby Chien posed for a photo with similarly dour looks on their faces. Artistic media can create formal equivalence where previously there was none; just as the word 'I' that I use to identify myself may refer to a quite different person from one moment or year to the next, the subject of a portrait may vary (from dog to human, for instance) yet retain certain qualities simply because of the medium or the style. The animal imagery in *I Am You* provides both a backdrop against which the human speaker's voice may be read and, through the eerie resemblance of animal expression to human expression in Tardos's work, allows for permeation between what we normally think of as natural—and all the strange meanings that accrue to the word—and what we think of as 'man-made.'

Such images are similar to the linguistic off-rhymes and morphings that occur throughout this book. Such morphings suggest that the way we conceive of agency, and thus the way we interact socially and politically, is largely formally determined. Our interactions are, by Tardos's account, a linguistic game, both totally crucial and comically playful: "I'm easily moved to tears./I'm tearily moved to ease./Eerily moved to tease."

If the phrase "to let go," to move on after a trauma, or give up after some sort of struggle, is a cliché, it is both something that the voices in these poems critique with such lines as "How can there be a universe in an ever-changing truth?" and, quite literally, the very occasion of these voices' existence. The "bloodbath" referred to in "The Letter: A Bloodbath" must be both the voices in the poem, as they critique the terms of their own existence, and a visceral thing. "The great surgery is underway and the patient is bleeding profusely," writes Tardos. The bleeding patient may be language as it is dismantled, but the 'patient' must also be people—particularly those who experience harm as a result of discourses that claim to help, heal, fix. Whether the president is able to coherently describe war using the same language that announcers use to describe baseball games, or whether we think of "misguided statesmen" or "statespeople" are questions of language-play with dire and bloody consequences.

"Letting Go" is dedicated "For M," and this dedication points up that the nature of generosity—of dedicating one's time and one's work—to a person or cause is circumscribed completely by the "ForM": by the formal practices and habits of one's speech or writing. The poems in this book tend to describe their own forms. One knows from the outset that "Letting Go" is a poem in 100 parts, and one is given ahead of time some patterns and themes to keep in mind. Just as this book describes itself as it moves along, it bears witness to your reading paths and habits as well. The voices in these poems issue their challenges ("On what terms am I the person I am?"), and as I read, my own responses seems to be continually echoed and recorded as the voices of the poems reflect on themselves. Think of *I Am You* as a public challenge to you as a subject, you as an 'I' and as a constant autobiographer: can 'I' conceive of myself as a monster, shifting and morphing through poetry, pop, politics, grief?

MARIE BUCK, Co-Editor, *Model Homes*

The Aim of All Nature Is Beauty

"My religion is to live—and die—without regret"
Tibetan poet saint Milarepa

In Memory of Jackson Mac Low

I. Introduction

I DO THE dishes
I double-click
I stand clear of the closing doors
Bottom-dollar gorgonzola

Bigelow jumping gigolo bump
An adventure.

The ganglionated arch of
Johann Gottlieb von Goodgirl,
who is really a very bad girl,
an angry girl, whose
almond-cake seduction via her
bocca, her thumbsucking bocca,
such a furious, pissed-off girl.

Her sibilant juicy sister, left alone amid all the senseless debris,
contemplates the schmerz of her lorgnette, her effortlessly
lovelorn fairy-tale suicide as she is pedaling in the darkness
that amplifies her task.

"Has she not made a scene?"
"No, she is not scenic."

Filial duties, artery cloggers.

You're right   I'm wrong   Whatever

Are you sure you're warm enough?
Try this visor if that one's too loose.
Please let me read my book in peace.
No, I'm not hungry today. I'll never be hungry again.
What's that smell? Is it food?

How come your feet are so big?
I can't stand it anymore.

Poor lonesome loon out on the lake, singing that mournful
    tune. All this rain is making me crazy. I would much
    prefer being lazy in the sun.

Motorists see more tourists see more hair

A certain pride   a certain dignity
A certain above-it-all that is genuine

Above the bickering the petty dusty petty lowly nasty little
    small-minded little beneath and little beneath

The agriculture of it all!
And the interactiveness of it all!

Topographically speaking a genuine representation of a
    human sentiment

The universe I inhabit versus the one that inhabits me

 The voice in the morning
 The first one to speak

Down a precipice

Off course

We need oblivion to escape oblivion
We need plants around us, and large pockets of time
wherein nothing much happens

Then maybe something can happen

II. Now That You're Gone

Now that you're gone

I can't read what I've written
I can't see it
I lost the ability to write
I can barely say my own name

 What happens now

What happens now can only be the result of everything
that has preceded this moment

This moment, the present, can only be seen as something
       that's very close to what has just been happening

The immediate memory of the just elapsed moment
is the closest we come to experiencing the elusive present

Immediate memory allows us to notice what our mental
processes have just been, and thus, becoming includes being

       Now that you're gone

Unrelenting-yearning-and-grief-consistently-benefitting-
       evidence-of-mental-reality-theorizing-small-pedestals-
       with-a-growing-and-grueling-exertion-facilitated-briefly

 Now that you're gone

Libertine gigolo vis-à-vis
Have a madeleine, it's good for the memory

Sedimentation fiber organism bedrock intensity lingo
formidable network realization flipside stratification data
delinquency meditation

Gotta be careful always

We're in the midst of an explosion and think it's just
everyday life

III. Intermezzo by a Lake

WE WERE HEADED for a cabin by a lake in a pine forest that
I had found on the Internet
All around us clockwork resolution happiness and conflict

We were headed for a cabin by the Internet of the lake
without a key to our consciousness

Headed as we were into an organizing notion of conflict and
happiness

We are sitting by a lake along the Internet, holding hands and
playing cards without a key

We are sitting at the window of a pine forest
Sitting in the lake of our happiness
Playing cards that we were given
holding keys in our hands
sitting on the notion of our minds within the years of
consciousness without a card
Holding hands

Headed to a cabin by a lake in a pine forest where we find each
other's happiness

IV. Going Away

MY LIFE TAKES time.
I realize that my life takes up a certain amount of time, which
   is the only reason I can refer to this particular state of
   being, as life.

He may go away.

Without the concept of time, I'd be like the animal that does
   not concern itself with labeling its life 'life.' It concerns
   itself with food and shelter and survival. This is good, it
   feels good, that, on the other paw, is bad. Not good.
   Don't go there.

He may be going away.

Temporal organization is of no conscious concern to the
   animal, although a cat will follow a very strict routine
   during the day, by preference.

He is going away.
But without a hierarchical agreement on temporal units and
   their applications, we could not have assembled here
   today.

He avoids going away.

Temporary eunuchs are an impossibility. The operation that
   produces a eunuch is irreversible. Did Greer, when
   coining the phrase "the female eunuch" imply that
   women's situation was hopeless?

He wants to go away.

From temporal units to temporary eunuchs. Sorry.

He may have gone away.

One question in writing could be: when do you hit the Enter
key and when do you not? When do you open a new
document? What do you call your file when you save it?
One option is to leave it Untitled1, Untitled2, etc., as in
emailing, when nothing is entered into the Subject field,
and the program volunteers the theme: "No Subject."
But such evasiveness has no virtue. When given an
opportunity to say something, say something!

He may be going away.

The difficulty can lie in integrating oneself into the
surrounding environment, for fear of losing one's
identity or individuality. And yet, of such a non-
assimilation, of a failure to accept being an integral and
vital part of the entire universe, nothing good will come.

He may avoid going away.

As usual, I return to myself with a sigh of relief.

He may want to go away.

My face needs to be animated by expression. My gaze should
be colorful, my smile defiant. I need to take a bath.
What am I waiting for? I'm used to my life. I talk to
myself out of a need to formulate my thoughts. A
woman presses her forehead against a mirror.

He has been going away.

To write. To face the blank page. Une feuille blanche, where blanc does not equal blank. A white page, or a blank document page on a screen, staring back at you blankly.

He has avoided going away.

The periodic need to note, to paint . . . to find that flexible, glistening, and fleeting adjective. It's an urge.

He has wanted to go away.

To be hungry and see oranges flung about.

He is avoiding going away.

We're OK together here, aren't we? Nothing to think about for years, just let life take care of everything. To think of nothing.

He is wanting to go away.

I recognize his impeccable looks and perfect pronunciation. Where will they lead me to? No one knows anything. I might as well be sitting on the moon.

He avoided wanting to go away.

To suffer, to regret, to prolong the night by insomnia, by solitary wanderings into the deepest, darkest hours of the night. I see it coming, yet I march bravely toward it. I hide my fears and tears with a dark eyeliner.

He may have been going away.

Nobody is waiting for me. I have no glory, no love, no money. No birds sing in the deep forest. How puzzling.

He may have avoided going away.

Years of marriage. A good chunk of my existence spent with a man who paints portraits of women, specializing in showing their velvety flesh. A scoundrel of the worst kind.

He may have wanted to go away.

My friends would say: well what did you expect, dear child, what did you expect?

He may be avoiding going away.

I had enough. The next day I didn't return and neither did I the next, or the one after that. And this is where my story ends, or rather begins.

He may be wanting to go away.

I won't dwell on the brief and morose period of transition that followed. There were consolations and felicitations. In any case I cut myself off and chose complete isolation, give or take a few close friends. My solitude is my freedom, which allows me to work hard.

He has been avoiding going away.

Sunday again. And how cold it is. My dog and I took our constitutional in the park after lunch. This animal will be my ruin. I spend more on her than on myself. But it's worth it just to be near her shiny coat glistening in the sun.

He has been wanting to go away.

Beautiful Sunday in a beautiful park. My dog and I think of this park as our own forest. She runs faster than I do, but then I walk faster than she does. A thin, pink haze filters the sun, a defanged sun you can actually look at. Flowers and mushrooms and violets in the grass on a bright winter day. I surge forward, feeling an elastic exhilaration and animalistic joy.

He is avoiding wanting to go away.

She is a born theatrical dog. She loves to run up on stage. I'm telling you all this so you understand her better. This is a dog who doesn't care about money, and who's been living in the garden—and in my heart—for a long time.

He may have been avoiding going away.

Extensive success and artistic ambition lead to silence, as does failure.

He may have been wanting to go away.

Nellie, a performing dog, drops by my dressing room. She seems to say to me, yes I know, you love me, you pet me, yes, you have a box of cookies waiting for me, but tomorrow or the day after, we're leaving and I probably won't see you again. So don't ask anything of me. The luxury of tenderness, peace, and security, is not available to the likes of me. Adieu then Nellie, adieu.

He may have been avoiding to go away.

Gertrude Stein: A vegetable garden in the beginning looks so
promising and then after all little by little it grows
nothing but vegetables, nothing, nothing but vegetables.

He may have wanted to go away.

So many things could go wrong, I'm afraid to ask. But a good
day can sneak up on you as unexpectedly as a bad one.
Silence in the garden.

He may go away.

My friends, the real ones, the faithful ones, are tied to me by
their solidarity. But I can hardly believe it. Friendship
should not be a ring through anyone's nose. Stripped by
some, hit on by others, you might want to imprison
yourself inside a gloomy serenity, made of incurable
goodness and silent contempt. Do not form that habit.

He has gone away.

The Nature of This Lecture Is
by John Beauty

This poem is an interweaving of linguistic elements taken from two sources: "John Cage," A Lecture by Norman O. Brown at Wesleyan University, February 1988; and "The Aim of All Nature Is Beauty," February 2005, parts I–IV, by Anne Tardos. Selections of the elements were made by making rapid inuitive decisions, as one would during a musical improvisation. Later, I refined the text, as I would in any editing process. It first appeared in the literary journal *Aufgabe #5*, edited by Tracy Grinnell.

This poem is dedicated too

(DACHINE RAINER)

His RELIGION IS to live without regrets

Due honor gratitude and a double-click

Wesleyan Zen Buddhism

       bottom dollar gorgonzola

Bigelow jumping gigolo bump

          John is at home

Musical duties and filial pedaling

       Revolution harmony

       Let me read my book in peace

Klikka-klakka on a beautiful day

As the representation of human sentiment

The first voice in the morning The first one to speak

          The one that says
          Yü = Enthusiasm

We need oblivion to escape oblivion

Noise is voilence
Conviviality is Eucharistic
Eating mammals is cannibalistic

Now that you're gone there is still your beauty

I can't read what I've written so I thicken the plot

I can barely say my own name and so I thicken the plot

Now that you're gone the enormous tragedy thickens the plot

Or was that soup?

We suffer history

Immediate memory of space and emptiness

Have a madeleine. It's good for the memory.

There is no spectator

We're in the midst of an explosion and think it's just everyday
life

The human race is one person

We are sitting on the notion of our minds within the years of
consciousness without a card, holding hands

Not disruptive, but cheerful

An interlude of farce or fooling

All around us clockwork resolution happiness and conflict

Noise is king and here comes everybody

My life takes time

A cat will follow a very strict routine during the day, by
preference

     He avoids going away.

Ritual clowns in primitive religion

     Not disruptive cheerful

He may avoid going away

     Apollonian sobriety and quietness in the face of
     Dionysian drunkenness

     Is life worth living   each day is excellent

To write.

     To be hungry and see oranges flung about.

Love's Body.

I return to myself with a sigh of relief.

Discipline discipline

Everything is taken literally, even silence

He may be avoiding getting rid of syntax, cadence, puns

Well what did you expect dear child, what did you expect

I stammered many years ago

My solitude is my freedom which allows me to work hard

Excessive success and artistic ambition lead to silence, as does failure

The anarchist dream of a noble individual

Circumstances

Silence in the garden

Love is fire

Never underestimate fire.

Fat Accomplice

In memory of Jackson Mac Low and Marcel Marceau

BROUGHT UP IN a post-modern relativist world
I cannot believe in direct messages — even from a text.

I can transpose one reality into another
". . . if I dream I have you, I have you."

I'm at my service yet I pay bare attention
I keep an open and soft mind and notice what's happening in
the moment
I am told that all things that arise have the nature to pass away
I believe this
It stands to reason
But there are other ways of looking at the same phenomenon
Impermanence can be seen as a vehicle of a process we call
becoming
I seek to find freedom in the way I relate to what's happening
in the moment.

You're almost always there

You're always almost there

I write silently as I try not to disturb the silence around me. I
become part of the silence and stop writing.

Can't Write

Blocked

blight
      bite

Blocked

bright
      light

           You became a blue light

         Something I could see one night

Brants broke our bric-a-brac
        In the bright light
           Took flight

Basic Logic for the Chinese Year of the Pig:

Every cat is animal.
Every pig is animal.
Therefore every pig is cat.

And every dog is not vicious.

A certain braveness comes into it after a while.

You can't force the issue

Anyway
It doesn't matter
Nobody cares
None of this is really happening

Take it from me.

None of this is really happening
Not to worry

Pick up the pieces
The thread

Barely a thought.

For a long time tongue tied
and speechless

Events in your life, my life, our lives
Events
Disappearing acts
Magic tricks
Heavy burdens

Each step of the way
Short bursts of thought
Ideas
Actions

In Paris once a long time ago
Before I was even there

I was there I was there
With and without friends
At different times
With different friends
Without any money
Often without enough food
I'd eat foie de morue from a can
That's cod's liver
In a can like sardines
Very oily and tasty
Good for a low budget
I'd eat it straight from the can without bread
Sitting on the edge of the bed
In the little room
Hungry
Alone
With my back to the world
And the world's back to me

Then it was going to be suicide by razor blade
But first a pantomime concert by Marcel Marceau
Then a proper meal in a restaurant, as a farewell gift, a final
        emptying of the purse.

The next morning, the blade pressing against the skin, unable
        to make the incision, waiting for the courage to do it,
        the doorbell rings.

It's a telegram. A Dutch film director wants to meet me under
the Eiffel Tower tomorrow for a documentary he is shooting on
young Parisians.

I show up and this man I had never met before gives me a
 bear hug
Then he suggests we do another take.
The Dutch crew records us hugging again.

Life continues.

Letting Go

A Poem in 100 Parts

Each page is connected to the next by the initial appearance of the phrase or the concept of "letting go," in its various forms.

The rest of the page is free.

(2007)

For M

1

IT'S THE EGO that lets go of the ego.
A leftist is usually right.
Everyone is really a very fine fellow.

I am an Acoustican.
I come from the planet Acoustica
Where we g'oham yeolnia ooh yeeanh
Some varsity sensibingatee zenifer lida
Shaka-ha-cha-ka!

Different papilla pamina different zugoria.

The standing the name the gesture
The movement
One cigale verisimilitude sentimentablement genial

Dissertation vegetation permission

A very fine fellow

2

THE EGG LETS go of the egg and becomes a bird
The bird appeals to our sense of freedom
and makes a cat salivate mentally
Cats don't salivate
Dogs salivate
Therefore dogs don't salivate mentally but actually
Birds don't salivate
I doubt they even salivate mentally

The killer instinct brushes its teeth at night
It flosses between its thoughts

Thoughts that create sounds
Sounds that become words

And words get along well with each other

Can't hold on to anything
ever
anyway
Not to the bird or the stone in your hand you would never
        throw at a bird

And all of this is really happening.

3

THE GIRL LETS go of the girl and becomes an adult
After a while, she will let go of herself and become something
     else
It's difficult to understand what
But I know that all of this is really happening
And that everyone is a very fine fellow

You confirm and you build by repetition
You invent a device that will repeat for you as needed

You hand a stone to a child and watch her break into a smile
The stone will remain calm and composed inside the little fist

The stone dreams of the beach
and of sandhood
The edge of the water where the children play

A play is by definition amusing
A muse is by definition a scantily clad young female floating
     about

4

A PENGUIN UNDERSTANDS the meaning of life just as a seal
   ends it.

Shilly-shally winter death
Monkey colorectum
Embrionic bazaar fracas
comprehension overcast

Cendrier Baudrillard
Upscale venison

Vertical severance
Digital mismatch

Empanades truc machin-chose
I chose to be the dingo

A pecking order in Beijing
to be
       to live
              to do
                     to give
                            to die

A cat, a sweetheart, maybe a baby.
In this case, maybe a koala.

5

THE EAGLE LETS go of the eagle
Its need to control reality causes its insomnia
Fear creates what is feared

Conversation scuba diddle
Verification jumble zig

Pretty little short supply
Glitter kindness gender gap
Delicate gene pool
Frisbee mutation
Unexpected peppermint

Razzmatazz

Thought exists.
Rigid necessity.

6

THE WRITER LETS go of intention and considers the
    alternatives

She is thinking about writing about thinking

Her imagination goes for a walk, along with her intentions
Arm in arm, the two walk around the block to get some
    exercise
They stop at a feminist sex shop and admire the toys on
    display
Then they buy a big bag full of pine-bark mini-nuggets at a
    garden supply store

They pay peanuts for the pine-bark mini nuggets, which they
    pour over their respective beloveds' graves

The writer tends to view most men as her feather

A feather seems lighter than air

How do you air a grievance? Is that anything like rhubarb?

Rhubarbs are to be enjoyed in moderation because of their
    high oxalic acid content. Calcium oxalate has been
    associated with the formation of kidney-stones because
    the calcium combines with oxalate in the intestines and
    this reduces calcium's ability to be absorbed.

Kidneys and stones will brake my bones
But beans will never hurt me

7

MY WINGS LET go of gravity and suddenly I'm flying

I soar higher than I would were I really up there

Fear of falling and hesitation are clear and understandable

That's right: fall we might

       From grace

          From paradise

Yes, she said, between pain and nothing I choose pain.

The promise of an imagined reality which may never happen

Is made up of desire
and
                     Great big pleasure

"So if I dreame I have you, I have you."

Something dark and murky here. Let me sweep off into
      another direction.

8

Sizable encounters let go of transformative stumbling
    blocks

The monster husband takes my hand

And it feels right

There is a definite thawing here

A melting and a charming company

My own charm

Not the charm my mother advised me to turn on as needed

More like an enchantment

Charm chant harm bent scant brant

Desire lifts me up just as a wave would

Easy to conjure up

and its power to lift is amazing

It hardly ever fails

I mean what *is* this?

9

Auto suggestion lets go of imagination and becomes
    reality

Reality is typically an invention within certain conventions

Conventions may become inconvenient when it comes to a
    coming together

Patience is counterintuitive yet helpful in moving from one
    moment to the next

Bypass the thrill of the shortcut, the coup, the disregard for
    universal order

Which soon fades in the face of another kind of thinking

Where you no longer look for certainty   you have arrived at
    your destination

10

Intense and prolongued anticipation will either let go of
        the monster husband's hand
Or tighten its grip around it and perhaps frighten it

The hand that feeds and bites
The self and the selfless
Always forward looking toward what has not yet happened.

The few things you can count on are not imagined or wished
        for

I
ache
hunger
throb
        pine
                burn
                        thirst
for you

I mean what *is* this?

11

THE MOMENT LETS go of the moment and suddenly past
    present and future are all one

We could get hurt by a misconstruction
Incorrect understanding
A clash
a breach
a rupture

and it's all over
and we're hobbling along on one leg pitifully

pride takes over
saving face becomes manifest

retreating to our respective caves
withdrawing fleeing vanishing

then comes the healing process
with its blisters and scabs and scars

leaving us disfigured and traumatized
bruised and defaced

Exactly that is the concern of the diffident "I"

12

Nothingness lets go of everything

The mind accommodates the body and it returns the favor
Calculating the extent and height of the sizable stumbling
       block that impedes progress
Or maybe just force the trajectory to take its proper course
Not propelled by hasty tempestuous reckless adventurism

So

Very grown up of you, in any case
Considerate and kind

But I mean what *is* this?

13

BATTLE FATIGUE LETS go of belligerence and pacifism sets in
Willy nilly.

Why does fear have to dominate everything?

I know that fear, like pain, has its use.

I understand that.

But let me think.

I'd like to know:

What exactly *is* this?

14

A SIZABLE HUSBAND takes my hand and then lets go of it
I tend to idealize the blows that come in my direction

Like the little girl in the arms of the nazi officer about to
carry her off to certain death
I look trustingly into the devil's eyes
I trust misfortune as much as happiness
It's not out of ignorance or dumb acceptance
But a form of compassion for even the most monstrous
ones among us

I romanticize your touch

Calvino suggests that we, humans, might be the eyes of the
universe through which it observes itself.

15

I LET GO of the idea of perfection and immediately find peace

Which brings me to that which I do

And for which I am responsible

I seem to be failing every test.
Nothing I do seems to quell anything
No amount of diversion diverts
No amount of aversion averts
Denial becomes ineffective
Nothing budges
It's like an antibiotic-resistant viral infection

I don't wish you to disturb me
You don't wish me to disturb you
All of which is disturbing

16

THE LIVING LET go of life and become dead
This gesture can plausibly be seen as a generous one

I can tell you a secret but I cannot show you my thoughts
I have no control over what I am objectively. Subjectively I am
    a "foot-loose, solitary, substanceless will."

As such, I am not content.

I realize that everything I say or do points to me.

"No one has ever loved anyone the way everyone wants to be
    loved."

17

THE INABILITY TO let go of an idée fixe is implicit in its
   nature.

You can take the monster's hand into your own and quickly
   let go of it.
The monster will be surprised at your own monstrosity and
   will make a horrible face.
You can reply in kind.
Grimace all you want.
Pretty soon one of you will start laughing and you'll be happy
   again.

The psychoanalyst plays the role of the ultimate competent
   observer.

Mary's little lamb loved Mary—followed her to school.

18

BUT THIS IS torture

The question is always who is doing the torturing
The father's ghost is never far away

How do I get out of this hole I fell into
Deep down inside where the air itself is scarce

It wouldn't be the first time:
I was once deemed too young
Now I am deemed too old
Or having too much baggage
Or coming on too heavily

What is this monster after?

19

AND WHY IS everybody a monster?

Is it because it's monstrous not to be happy?

Even to be hungry and masticating and digesting strikes me as
    monstrous

The monster father's ghost, hidden inside my monstrous
    psyche

I demand to be loved
I make it a condition
This too is monstrous

"Pull down thy vanity
I say pull down."

To find lightness

Then you take a deep breath. (You might as well do it right
    now.)

20

I CAN'T LET go of my constant companion
the iPod
it tells me exactly what I want to hear
Whispering it into either ear

All it needs is some of my power

I have enough to spare
Too much for some
Hardly any
in reality

Those who fear my power would fear anything

But enough of scary monsters hiding under the bed already

21

DO NOT LET go of the swift instinct of self-preservation, the
    deepest of all the automatic instincts.

A certain blind pathetic forcefulness of life.

One meaning blotting out another.

Friendship exactly.

A certain quickness of impatience.

And now, in a world gone gray and baboon-like, you made
    everything baboon-horrible with your baboon lips and
    grimaces.

22

L ET G O O F the growing process and watch the withering

As all of this unfolds
I am losing *love* and gaining *like*

If you've been adored as a small child, you would probably
    understand

It is the child who is unfaithful
radical and daily transformations followed by eventual
    departure

A man who fulfills all the needs and forgives all the faults
lover, friend, teacher, son, and grandmother.

What luxurious protection love has offered
Love means "I'm not only yours, I *am* you. I shall live for you."

Our cat Roof
lived for us

She lived exactly as long as was required.

        If indeed it is an ending.

23

WANT TO BUT can't let go of thinking of you
There is a yearning that borders on the unhealthy
Or else I don't understand what's happening

"As soon as I name, I am named."
(As soon as I maim, I am maimed.)

It's all true.
This emotional mess I am in
This humiliating debasing degrading pathetic
This pitiable wretched condition
This abyss

24

THERE IS NO way out of one's own obsessions, be they
    anticipatory or baseless,
it's futile to attempt any letting go of them.

This kind of eroticism has to do with preparation
The actual act would be a disappointment
A deflating experience
This is about Desire, not Pleasure

Sensually produced significance

Roland Barthes: Why should emotion be antithetic to bliss? It
    is a disturbance, a bordering on collapse: something
    perverse, under respectable appearances emotion is
    even, perhaps, the slyest of losses, for it contradicts the
    general rule that would assign bliss a fixed form: strong,
    violent, crude: something inevitably muscular, strained,
    phallic.

What did you just say? I could hear your voice, but couldn't
    get the words.

25

IF THIS HELL won't let go of me, it must be because
I don't want it to.

Insistence is suffering

"Strong, violent, crude: something inevitably muscular,
    strained, phallic."
Something has to take the place of Pleasure

The drive demands it
The demand drives it

Every hint of a possibility of pleasure immediately sends
    sparks of anticipation
Up the spine of this misguided, mistaken, misdirected
    phantasmagorian

26

THE MORE I try to let go of this quicksand
The deeper I sink into it
Until I have no choice but to perish in this grotesque death trap

Nietzsche said that a tree is a new thing at every instant. We
affirm the form because we do not seize the subtlety of an
absolute moment.

Was the original, German . . . *die Feinheit eines absoluten Momentes?*
Does anybody know?

The back-translation is by Babelfish, with my somewhat
halfhearted approval.

27

I'M BOUND TO let go of this boundless energy
I have fallen in love with someone who can't face it
The only thing he can think of is to not call
To not contact

What an idea!

It might give him a sense of importance, I can well imagine
     such comforts

My defeat is all I have to offer
It's all he accepts from me now
I gladly expose myself to that
Masochistically
Oh so masochistically

But don't think I'm enjoying this pain, unlike the count von
     Sacher-Masoch, converting pain into pleasure—I'm just
     hurting like a wounded animal.

28

I CANNOT CONTROL what's happening to me

I don't like what's happening to me

Sadness looms again
In a different form
An endless confirmation of my solitude
My enormous loneliness

I miss you like a drowning man misses his lifeline
A drowning woman. Drowning, in any case.

29

D ROWNING PLEASANTLY
Drowning in pleasantness
Drowning
Going down
Giving up
Letting go
Reflecting on futility

Fruit.

Cyclical nourishment

At night, I would write for the morning

30

ALORS NOUS CRÉONS ensemble
We work together whether we know it or not
We're all part of the same Salon:

Every Tuesday at five
Doused in perfume

The smell of fear is gone, but its memory lingers

Lingering lollipop fingering
Dizzying figuration

Sad and lonely creatures help each other sometimes
They know what it's like
They're being gentle

31

WE'RE CAREFUL WITH each other now that we're dead
Now that we're dead we are more gentle

We're dead because death has touched us by taking our
    spouses
When my spouse dies, I die

When my spouse dies, I cry

I wonder what's happening

It's difficult to understand this transformation
This disappearance act
This magic trick

Now you see me and then I don't

32

No AMOUNT OF letting go seems enough

That some people seem to care that I exist surprises me

I always assume I am not loved
As my parents trained me to be

My parents.
Don't get me started.

You spoke to me lovingly tonight for the first time
You seem solitary somehow diminished

33

NOT YOU.
I speak to, and of, different people

I transform myself into someone new
She wants to be liked

There will be a lot to edit out tomorrow morning, assuming I
   wake up and walk to my desk where I sit down and
   think

I made it.
It's the next morning and I am here, reading what I wrote last
   night.

My knife isn't as trigger happy as I had anticipated.

34

YOUR KNIFE IS a lot sharper
Cuts deeper, like a Samurai's sword
Your swing is determined and unwavering

In one hand you hold a scalpel
In the other

I hate to think

The blood is dripping from your hands copiously
Is that what you want?

That red pool at your feet is slippery
Be careful

This is some sort of kosher butchering
I know

Let the victim slowly bleed to death
Perish at your feet as if in a faint

Then what? You boil my carcass and devour it at your next
    meal?

Incorporating your own murderous sins through my remains?

No doubt, it's what I allow to happen.

35

I CAN'T LET go of the notion that something is terribly amiss
No blame
just a sense of certainty that this
whatever "this" is
is off
and askew

Why I should be perceived as a threat is beyond me

"But negation is affirmation by denial of a repressed wish.
        Freud 1925"
            If you left off the "repressed wish" part of the
                sentence, it would still be useful.

36

To HELP ME let go of you
I need to focus on your faults
How devoid of compassion

Compassion is a prerequisite for decent living
For oneself
Little animals
One's own thoughts

It is what allows universal harmony to come about

You're mistaken to think you have no hand in it

We are all responsible

This is a group effort
That's why it's impossible to bypass politics

We're all in this together

I want to blame you but I can't

37

IN LETTING GO of you I let go of unmistakable happiness

It wasn't a fluke, it was real
Now we're back to everyday life

How could you refuse such a gift

I have to admire your determination, however misguided.
Your strength.

Like the mouse who is being destroyed by the cat, can't help
but for a brief moment, admire the cat's power.

"This behavior won't stand," you said of yourself, yet as you
can see, it stands firmly.

This is killer behavior.
I have never encountered the like.

Most impressive in its fierceness.

38

I LET GO of the idea of writing a poem for you

Dark green, geometrically formed eaves in front of my
        window
The color of a lake.
The eaves are solid and steadfast

Is it time for me to go swimming?
The problem is that I am a good swimmer

I don't want to kill anyone, including myself

Sometimes I think that you should be ashamed of yourself
Which you probably are

39

I FEEL SHAME too.
Shame is a big thing around here. The shame-blame shell
  game.

As when precious food is being destroyed while many go
  hungry

Because of some disbelief

A certain kind of callousness points to your own suffering

As you splash about in tepid mediocrity
Eternally
Safely
Hopelessly

40

THE PURPLE TREE on the roof across the street
The one behind the dark green eaves
Has let go of its purpleness and has turned green

I like to think of this transformation as the "way of the world"

You say you're melancholy.
Well *might* you be.

You chose melancholy over ebullience. It's what you had
        ordered.

I do all that's required: reach out to friends, see people, go out
        a lot

Nothing
        nothing
                nothing
                        helps.

41

NOTHING I'D RATHER do than let go of this feeling.
Not one blessed thing
Give me a way out, throw me a lifeline
I'll grab it, boy.
Help.

I had it easier with my good friend and ally by my side

But this
This
This is different
Completely different kind of attraction

New to me
Exhilerating and uplifting

Sure I lost my cool, but did you have to abort the entire baby-
    bathwater for that?

42

AT ONE POINT, I remember, you made a difficult phone call
You called me and said
Just take it easy
it's going to be alright

that was good advice
I should have taken it, but I didn't
And neither did I take it easy
Is that any reason to abort the entire baby-bathwater?

Now I must go back to forming those spiral galaxies

43

WE COMMUNICATE BY not communicating
We ride some waves

Vibes, man, vibes . . .

I can't get involved in other people's lives
Their fortresses are firmly in place
I'm not in warrior mode (mood)

Some people tacitly agree that they have nothing to fear from
    each other.

Those are the ones I want to be with.

The exposure is savage.
Everything is wildly out in the open.

Yet:
"The beloved's desire takes precedence"

or:
"Please don't leave!"

44

YOU KNOW WHAT ? Fuck you!

A nonexistent relationship still exists as such, as long as it is
    acknowledged, even in the negative. (negation is
    affirmation by denial)

Peut être

She praised him by saying "Oh you're so brutal!" He seemed
    pleased. He was not her son, and she was not his
    mother. They played mother and son, but they were
    lovers. I don't know how to play that, although I
    understand the game. I can sympathize.

Games. Who needs them.
Apparently we do. Without them the flow would be unruly.
    The game acts as a defining structure where borders and
    limitations are created in favor of a more efficient, more
    rationally directed flow. A structure that sets up that
    which is to be done. The artist can help things along a
    bit.

The next move is to consider one's own honor. (honorably)

45

THIS SADNESS GET Over.
This Sadness Let Go.

The trend toward acceleration grows at exponential speed.

Distancing becomes an integral part of the process.

Momentum generates new patterns of motion

Pusillanimousness goes unrewarded.

What's a structuralist to do?
Is Freudery an Embroidery?
A decoration?

Everything rotates around the enormous struggle it is
to get from one moment to the next

Everything we do and say is structured around this struggle

And to ease the passage

with more confidence,

language is being used

46

LET THE TIDE flow

until an idea occurs

Let music induce emotions

Let art play this role in human life

Any sense of crisis is due to an upsurge in individualism

There is no single way
except what leads to death
and as long as the organism can modify itself, change its ways,
    it avoids death.

I feel singularly vulnerable today.

I want to shrug it off. Wait it out. Let it pass.

47

THE DOOR HAS reopened a crack

But I no longer trust you. I know what you're capable of. (And
for what?)

Still, the door has reopened a crack, and this celebration
borders on sadness. Your preferred mode. Your charm is
greatest when you break through your enormous
tristesse. The most liberating smile ever.

It comes unexpectedly like a sudden breeze. You are happy
and making everyone around you happy. It's miraculous.

Then you turn it off and close the door behind you.
You hide out somewhere and we're left on the outside,
wondering where you'd gone.

We accept this as your character, as who you are.

We tread carefully and don't wish to hurt you with anything.
We're not sure what would hurt you but it's clear to us
that you're expecting to get hurt.

We try to protect you as we love you.

48

SOME OF US are tough old birds, others delicate little flowers
I could be either or both, now that I'm living, now that I'm
     alive
After all

For a moment there, I wasn't sure how soon all this would
     end, but now it's back to not having a clue, which is the
     way we like it. We, humans.

I want to be the goddess of memory and eyesight, and be
     awash in mental powers.

Until they too disappear and I'm back in the frogpond

Being idle and pondering could be at the root of inspiration —
     or not.

An idea can come out of the blue, or you can coax it

As in love making

49

"11:30 PM

Maybe too late to call.

But I got your message(s) and Yes, Saturday is good.

Come anytime you like."

How can this be? There is no such person in the world as me.
I'm inventing this person I am continually becoming. By
collaborating in this drama, you co-author it. You
cultivate the myth.

We playact who we are. We pretend all the time. And what
happens when we drop the act? Who are we then? The
ones to ask for directions.

Delusional fantasy infringing on so-called reality, eliminating
the need for any action.

50

You must have lived your life in a desert.

Turned into something of a stone
Petrified

But the stone dreams of the beach
and of sandhood
The edge of the water where the children play
Remember?

Such monstrosity must be resisted.
I can't walk into a place that practically guarantees to make
me suffer.

And we've seen the previews.

Besides, I couldn't sway you to sway with me.

51

WILL I LET go of this poem and move on to another one?
Why should I?
Is there something wrong with this poem?

Self-reference is usually frowned upon.
So be it.

I'll go to a hundred.
Then I'll stop.
Stop what?
This.
And what is this?
I have no idea.

Words fly like bullets tonight.
I shoot myself in the foot with them.

I try and make good use of what life throws at me.

52

I THINK THAT we recreate our childhood experiences in order
to relive the exhileration and euphoria of those days.
The quality of the experience seems completely
irrelevant. It's the association we're after.

This page cannot be a refuge
No page is an island . . .

Should you find me the wrong gender, think strapon.

Yes, strapon. Sounds like tampon. Looks and feels like penis.
Without any of your imagination
Or the warmth of your skin

I can't imagine where I was going with this. The closer I come
to my destination, the farther I seem to back away from
it.

Two children
We play together

In the (radioactive) sand

We embrace that stuff

53

A CONVERSATION CAN go on, long after it has been
    terminated.

"I adore you, darling, but I'm not all there, you know."

"Adore you to death."

A virtual, voyeuristic life that requires the telling, or
    conveying, of another's experience—second hand

The courage required to leave this loft is legendary.

The courage it takes to leave this loft is legendary.

54

LETTING GO OF the ideal, making mistakes, getting both
 hands dirty

I am past caring, you know, yet I have never cared more.

"Find a man who defends you against other men. Do not play
 with the vile animal (the monster). Do not release it."

I feel I'm getting into a mess by coming out into the open
By coming out into the open, I find myself ever more unsure
 and vulnerable

You offer your arm, listen, and give advice
It's what we do for each other

55

PRECIOUS HUMAN BEINGS let go of their precious human
   bodies

You have nothing to fear from me

For one thing, we can't be

So there won't be anything and therefore there won't be
   anything
I already got hurt amid all this nothing

Why would I want more?

I'm finding out about how much grief I can take
Lost two cats: one feline and one human.

At first it's the death you need to deal with
That incomprehensible act
It's all fine and good for you to be dead, but how am I to carry
   you about?

After three years, I'm getting used to it, you're not heavy
And I also realize that I no longer stand on the same ground I
   stood with you.

56

LET GO OF the firm ground and grind to a halt (or freely fall)
There was never any certainty
Things were in constant flux
We never knew when it would all end
So it always ended. It ended daily.
When the end finally came it was a dread fulfilled
Satisfying in an odd way
Like the criminal, who feels relief after confessing to the
    police.
It's finally over.

The dying itself was a very private affair, but I couldn't spare
    you the hospital torture. I'll never get over that one.
    Dying can be shitty.

Nothing is like it had ever been
I'm in completely unknown territory now

Friends assure me that their friendship is the same
But I am not the same

I don't want to be the same
I couldn't survive

I had to change into someone who no longer needs you
Someone who could get through all this
You have become someone I carry around
We are wearing different costumes now.

57

I WOULD DON a strapon for you and enter you from behind
Give you the oxygen you need
Pleasure would make you inhale deeply
I would be delighted
I would be

Now
In this ocean of life

Yet this sudden idea of your possible gayness
Instead of being a relief, saddens me

Suddenly saddens.

So am I the wrong gender
Is that it? Oddly, not a relief.

Because gay does not mean not sleeping with women
Not gay does not mean not sleeping with men

But not sleeping with anyone means being alone

As I am

58

You're flattered that I inquire about your sexual
    orientation
You're amused by it
Better than incredulity and self deprecation

Maybe you're right. Maybe I should look elsewhere for a
    certain kind of thrill, and keep you as my friend and
    confidant, tell you about my conquests and defeats. Cry
    on your shoulder and have you console me. Chéri.

Is that what you want?
Dear.
The beloved's desire takes precedence.

59

LET'S GO AND find out what it is that *I* want.
I like the absurd and the impossible
A distorted take on beauty maybe

This worries you because you fear that I will underline your
    own absurdity

You may be right to fear that
I'm operating on a fairly perverse premise
Not the most ethical of premises

You are right to mistrust this impulse, and I shall back off.

Here we are: frozen in fear and perversion

You think they'll say "Can't imagine what s/he sees in
    him/her."
And since when do we care what "they say"? (Since always.)

suffered much humiliation in life
like too much.

Take that into consideration. The closer we get, the more we
    become responsible for each other.

Snared and entangled in a self-perpetuating matrix of human
    attractions, we prop each other up.

60

RELIEVED TO HEAR you say you're heterosexual.
And "to the bone," yet.

That puts me back into the running. There is still a chance for
    me then.
A chance to make you suffer and see you squirm as I punish
    you for having had the temerity to resist me.

Am I still the little girl who smashed frogs against bricks just
    to see what would happen?

I maintain that you have nothing to fear from me.
I haven't lived all these years without evolving. What I did to
    the frogs, I got back in spades.

Elsewhere, it says: "Three uninvited guests arrive. Honor
    them, and in the end there will be good fortune."

Even unexpected people and events are honorable.
Everything and everyone matters. Everything we say and do is
    important and will have consequences. This gives us
    some control over what happens.
It's a good thing.

61

Now that there is a glimpse of a possibility of seducing you
More exactly, submitting to you
I see that it's the last thing I would want

It's all wrong

Sexy on the phone — the male voice

And that one time we shook hands in the subway
When I got off at Franklin Street

That handshake

It was quick, lasted about a second or two.

That amazing handshake

62

SUDDENLY, THE DOOR shut in my face. I quickly let go of that
one.

Nearly all door re-openings that have taken place, have been
due to my intervention.

When promted, you respond well, erotically, cheerfully—
unless my come-on is paranoia-laden. Then the door
quickly closes.

I'd say who could blame you, but I won't say it because I want
to blame you.

Yet, why should I blame you for being who you are?

But also: why should I submit to you?
What do I want here? To coax you out of your shell, and then
what?
Do I expect great things? No? Do I expect pleasures?

It just occurred to me that I might be hoping for just that.

Also, I should mention that this could be called the Age of
Typesetting, since so many humans now set type.

63

THE TRUTH IS that I love you I love you I love you
Yes, of course it's madness, of course I'm crazy
Of course it's impossible and of course I'm being difficult

Yes yes yes I know and yet I love you

You don't trust my excentricity, and yet I love you.

Nothing could ever come of an "us," still, I love you

I want to touch you, feel you, moving slowly, tenderly
I long for you   and I love you

But I don't know where you are. I can hardly see you. I see
        your pain, it's in your face; I see your sensual body.

Once I felt your hand in the subway. It was magical.

There are many hands and bodies, and I had to fall for yours,
        with your mountains of issues.

Like I *need* this?

64

I LET GO of the idea of
hostile neglect
It was just indifference.

And to another You:
Sometimes I feel like I am betraying you by being alive
And then I feel you are betraying me by not being
The truth is that both—and even neither—are true.

And the truth doesn't always work.

Suddenly I've become venerable
I would much prefer to play in the mud with the other
froggies.

Who is this honorable person I'm supposed to be?
Fuck that.
Let's just relax.

65

YES, I THINK, between grief and nothing, I will take grief.

Because of my keen sensitivity to the tragic transience of
things, the concept of an emergency contact—and
contact would have been the thing.

Strong perfume says both: Come Here and Stay Away.

I just like the smell. (Wagner used to order different perfumes
for different operas, as he wrote them.)

You create the atmosphere in which to work.

66

I THOUGHT I had a pineapple around here somewhere, but I
    must have lost it.
Now I have no pineapple.
This happens a lot.
Sometimes I go for a long time without a pineapple.

I could pick one up at the corner store anytime.
But I try to not always get me what I want.
Keeps me on my toes

It's as if the moment had passed.
Maybe even the ship has sailed

I plan to be there for you, doing what friends do for each
    other, selflessly, admirably, lovingly.

Deep solitude alternating with rich social interactions
meaningful exchanges of thoughts
and other nonverbal impulses around the room.

Shoo, stupid boy, shoo.

67

It's not the letting go that hurts. It's the holding on.

I am deeply and erotically yours

And still, you can't fire me because I quit!
Oh that's right. You never hired me in the first place.
How could I forget.

68

SOMETHING ABOUT LETTING go of sexual fantasy and
    excitement, I forget what.

Denial can fuel desire

She said that it was a bit s&m of me to submit to someone I
    don't like
She probably meant m, not s. M is the s. He slaps me around.
    Lets me know who is boss.

Deviation is good.
Distance, absence, all good things.
Must let go of this particular one—.
I'm lost, absent, alone, right now.

The cat, making for the door, says to the woman: "I'm going
    out now. Do you need any voles?"

Stripsody.

69

So it's back to syntax, is it? Letting go of experimenting
with language and returning to meaningful sentence
structures? It can happen.

She may be the horniest poet of our time.
And one of the bravest and wisest, they say.
They honor her while she throws up.
They admire her.
This makes her want to throw up even more, and so on.

She adores to listen to almost anything Thelonius Monk ever
recorded.

70

MANY FISH SWIM by here.
They all say to me "As long as the body holds out."

They speak to me of a tedious dying process, followed by a lot
of nothing, which is supposed to be a relief after all this
something.

They say they count on being flexible about the whole thing
and hope to make a smooth transition. They know they
are capable of being good about such events.

The young support it.

An olive. Actually, nine, black olives. Shiny.

Don't look for hidden meanings.

71

As soon as the spirit lets go of the body, it begins to
    decompose.

Nothing can touch or be touched, except the body.

And while everyone is very sensitive, that's not a fault.

The only way to get through life is to love it.

LET GO OF the idea that we're not sitting on the Beach of the
Future. We are.

The beach is a given. Where else would we be? In a parking
lot?
I think not.
This is definitely a huge, sandy beach.
The ocean is everything that we're not.
It's external, it's enormous, and we barely understand it.

the beach is a given
the future is also given
we're in it

this is the Beach of the Future

Relax, enjoy the scene.

73

Being difficult so people will let go of the idea that I
    might be easy?

These are tough questions.

A complete stranger most of the time, which is why we
    couldn't even be friends.

I'd break down you either hold my hand

I'm always inclined to want to improve on a situation

74

I LET GO of the belief that you are not twisted and perverse.
    You are.

Real lonely monsters are cutting into dreams to speak what
    isn't believed.

Just touching, they float until they feel something.

Unable to speak, the monstrous loner swims into hiding.

We all have our own particlar brand of cheerfulness.

Intense ways.

75

THE CHANNEL IS open. Avail yourself of it.

What a dirty plum of a monster.
Sweetheart, I just can't deal with your flair for drama
I'm sorry
What's that? What did you say?

Well, either way. So long, kid. I adore you to death. Goodbye,
    goodbye.

How little it takes for you to treat me as a complete stranger

No amount of appeal seems to sway your cold heart.

It's not even cold. It's absent.

It must be hell in there.

What I love is love.
Real friendship.
Not this.

Devastating charm and heartlessness.
Do women like to be mistreated? Hell no!
Not this one, and not any others I know.

76

DON'T JUST KEEP letting go of everything.
You need to hold on to certain principles, ethics, morals.

I don't like boys who play rough
You are brutal, and I won't praise you for it

Your work should have tipped me off
This is a deep dark heavy kind of brutality

The kind I'm happy not to know too well
And to think I wanted you.

I want you.

Gone.

77

I'M LETTING YOU go.

I'm being judged and condemned, and very nearly executed.
Although that part would have to be done by sepuku
(harakiri). What you offer up is like a bad dream.

Basically a lowlife.

Imgaine *me* making such a mistake? The old girl finally lost
her touch.
Whaaah? That guy over there? You're kidding!
No, I'm telling you, she writes in her poem that she fell for
this guy who doesn't wanna know from her, at least not
the way she does.

No, really. Poor thing. But she looks good. Has she lost weight?
Looks like it. Also, did you notice, she dresses better
than heretofore?

Did you say "heretofore?"
Yes, that's what I said. Now, where was I?
Something about letting go of you.

78

WHAT MORE CAN you let go of, after you've let go of
everything?

Oh yeah, baby, I do drama, bigtime

Deal with it

However intimately vice

Comedy is a game that imitates life.

The comic is accidental.

Laughter appears to stand in need of an echo.

79

AND NOW YOU have declared something new

You want to see me

As soon as possible

You feel something

You send a sweeping message

After a week of leaving my messages unanswered

Then the tedious apologies

Yeah yeah yeah

80

I DON'T KNOW what's more rude: phoning someone or
    emailing them
I should use a lot more discretion in my communications

I can't wait to see you again
So it's a romance after all
Now I'm scared

Because, well
Just plain scared

Pure as a young bird
As a patch of moss
A sudden breeze messing with your hair

But enough of these profanities.

81

IT'S TIME TO let go of the narrative section of this poem and
    let the ride begin

Haa-ooh-aah

M M M M M M M M M M M M M M M M M M M M M M M M
M M M M M M M M M M M M M M M M M M M M M M M M
M M M M M M M M M M M M M M M M M M M M M M M M
M M M M M M M M M M M M M M M M M M M M M M M M

Won't you be my silicone doll
Won't you be my forever stamp
No I will not fix your computer

Music You
Possibly

82

IT'S GOOD TO leave some air between lines, but not too much.
The touch should be light.

The light should be touching.

Forgiveness borders on religiosity.

This is a verbal-visual composition, relying on typography.

This Is the Age of Type on the Beach of the Future.

Fee-uuu-ture.

The perception of change.

83

Releasement and thinking.

Each thought is too short.

Resistance can be the result of a lack of skill.

"Development of intellect alone is not sufficient, very soon work on emotions becomes necessary."

"When you find negative emotions in yourself, you must understand that the causes are in you and not in other people—the causes are internal, not external."

Mindfulness and
Self-remembering

84

Now it's my turn to exercise caution.
After the: "I don't promise much, but this I promise…"
I need to make sure I'm not making a mistake

How flaky is it?

Your seductive invitation to be happy is preceded by
      something about the bottom of your heart.

Careful now.

I require certain standards. High maintenance, you know.

You pay for what you get.

EvM: You pay for every breath you take.

85

OR I COULD just fuck you and then let you go
Send you on your merry way

I may or may not know what others think
I have to assume certain things
Observe the world around me

Time is smiling at me today

Imagining us together feels good

Something about you I detest
It's something inside me that I detest
I may detest men. And women.

86

I THINK IT'S too late to let go now

Without going off the deep end, as you say
Good advice I'll try to follow

"I like you kid, but don't get your hopes up too high." Very
    Humphrey Bogart Philip Marlowe Hollywood and Vine.

Fair enough

Everything is sacred and holy—don't let go of that

87

Now that Eros has draped itself around us

We can let go of previous torments and face new ones

Sindbad diligent tango
Zinfandel infantilism fright
Every life form a work of art
Tango diligence lovely emotion

> Work-of-art life form
> Internal emotion tango
> infantilism lovely fright
> work-of-art Sindbad zinfandel

Surprising devotion enthusiasm
Uncomplicated approach
Unafraid at last and no more secrets
Secretions turn us inside out

88

I LET GO OF everything else and devote myself to my work
Now that they let me

We're going to be very close friends who once used to fuck

It's not that we only use 10% of our mental capacities—we use
   them all. It's language and what it covers of the human
   experience that's limited to ten percent.
.

Origen: There are certain things, the meaning of which it is
   impossible to adequately explain by any human
   language.

My heart is bursting with an emotion that stings

Right now I'm learning how to write
All over again
Don't know why
It's just happening

89

I HAVE DIFFULTY letting go of the idea that we all basically
detest each other and that love and friendship are states
in which we temporarily escape the animosity. An oasis
of sentiments.

Seduction by email
Can you imagine?
Everybody does it.

"Children around the world put camel shit on the walls"

That corny, elegant tango.

90

LET GO OF looking for significance in everything
If everything is significant, nothing is.
If every hair or blade of grass matters then nothing matters.

I trust you.

"Shigedah bath, really a sign of haaaa…"

I Love Serious Artists.

The green matrix has its delicate green tentacles firmly inside
my ear canal. The matrix is cleverly friendly. I am aware
of the creepy bodily invasion while I listen to piano
sonata number 30 in E, op. 109: gesangvoll mit innigster
empfindung (andante molto cantabile et espressivo).

91

MUCH TO LET go of still
We're not at the end yet
This could be a beginning
In which I would have a voice
I would be heard and listened to
A beginning and a continuation in which I would be taken
    seriously and believed and listened to and heard and
    understood and trusted

92

AFTER ALL, I could have been messing with your head. You
    had to make sure that I wasn't.
I had to meticulously and elaborately prove to you that I am
    good, honest, and kindhearted, which is problematic
    because I could have been messing with both our heads.

Monsters under the bed.

Ah, to be happy again.
"Happy in America."

Buddha driver
Motion encourages motion
Buddha driver

That beaming smile on the faces of new lovers: it's happiness.

Can I really achieve the lightness I seek?
The answer can only be: yes, but you won't be able to hold on
    to it
Deal, as in "it's a"

"Perfection has its price."

93

BUDDHA WANTS A word:
You must let go of lightness as soon as you have found it.

Eros pulled us together.
Let's see what pulls us apart.

I run a feather over your skin
Softly teasing the monster inside you
Watching you defeat it (tame it)
Enjoying the gentle touch

As I was leaving the studio, you rushed over and asked me
what I was listening to on my headphones. When I said
Django, you had a sudden outburst of love for life, for
Django, for me.

94

THERE WILL BE the greatest of difficulties to let go of
You know that. There always are.

I am good, honest, and kindhearted, but if I can imagine
    disasters, they already become a distinct possibility.

Not just disasters, but constant and recurring doubts,
    heavinesses, ridicule—by whoever—probably me. (Fear
    creates what is feared.)

You know it's eros when your knees weaken at the thought of
    the lover.

95

LETTING GO : SELF nature
Essence neither leaving nor staying

Just let things be and you will walk freely and undisturbed.

Rest and unrest derive from illusion.

With enlightenment there is no liking and disliking.

Released from all entanglements.

With a single stroke we are freed from bondage
Nothing clings to us and we hold on to nothing

When doubt arises, just say "not two."
In this "not two" nothing is separate nothing is excluded

A book of Nothing. Hsin Hsin Ming.

96

I'VE BECOME EXACTLY the person to whom I had always been
attracted, the person I was hoping to become. The
soothing, comforting perfume, evoking god-knows-
which grownup that seduced me as a child.

Our voices know and recognize each other.

97

ITEMS YOU ARE not allowed to ship to Germany via the
United States Postal Service:

Absinthe.
Arms and weapons.
Articles bearing political or religious notations on the address
side.
Human remains.
Live plants and animals.
Melatonin.
Perishable infectious biological substances.
Playing cards, except in complete decks properly wrapped.
Pulverized coca beans.
Radioactive materials.

LET GO OF your copyright
It will have to be alright
Let go of the lover so he doesn't feel confined
It will be fine

Gotta be careful — always.

The question is always how to best spend every moment
of every day.
Would I know it if I lost my mind?
Depends on the particular kind of dementia I'd be
suffering from
I would imagine one might suspect in some cases

My elders show me what's waiting for me around the corner.
Why do pigeons exist?
Quiet bahnhof.
And exactly how close should we come to another?

Rottweil.

99

GOOD MOOD JUST won't let go of me.
Lurking under the surface
Waiting for any excuse
Slightly idiotic seeming.

A horse shakes his head near Heidelberg

Is this optimism or happiness?

Lightness around Stuttgart.

Ustinov: *Le rire est la musique la plus civilisée du monde.* Laughter is
the world's most civilized music.

ONCE YOU SINK your teeth into something you don't
    let go easily

We're crossing Germany to Switzerland at Singen. (to
    sing)

Three border patrolmen aggressively search an Arab-
    American man's luggage and then walk away,
    saying "Nice to meet you" without looking at my
    passport, which I will need to renew soon.

May your elegance outweigh your cruelty.

The poem is a sculpture I model, chisel, shape.

Train to Oerlikon, in which the commuters hang upside down
    in the compartment like giant bats.

The sense of urgency in love has to do with the lover not
    wanting to waste precious time.

In love making, frankly, you're a little rough
A tad rough
Just a tad

Itt ülök csillámló sziklafalon
(Here I sit on the glistening palisade)
[IT-ulok TSHILL-ahmlow CYCluh Falon]

Chill am low baby
Way out.

The Letter:

A Bloodbath

A Poem in 50 Parts

Each page begins and ends with a question.
The rest of the page is free.

(2007)

"Where am I? Who am I? How did I come to be here? What is
this thing called the world? How did I come into the world? Why
was I not consulted? And If I am compelled to take part in it,
where is the director? I want to see him."

— SOREN KIERKEGAARD

1

AND WHAT'S THE deal with losing it once you're inside?
Mouth good, cunt not? Is that it?

Don't know if happiness is the ultimate goal here,
but it's a good guideline.

Risk is said to be the essence of life.
Meditation is said to be a serene encounter with reality.

On the other hand, I'm not wild about the way you touch me. A
bit rough and not with discernable pleasure.
If you don't get off on going down on me, then why do it?

I'm easily moved to tears.
I'm tearily moved to ease.
Eerily moved to tease.
Sheepishly moved to wheeze.
Weepily wooed to breeze.

Scintillating Andromeda.

Too avant garde for any arrangements.
Too distracted to come.

Is that how we are?

2

ART AS A form of insanity?
Only in the most twisted sense.

Saxophone t-shirt tourism pigeon-shit.

Violent conflict is needed to create a spark.

I forgive the cat for killing the mouse. It is written.

The fly is welcome too, as long as it behaves.

You move around in realms that are familiar to you.
They make you feel secure. One might say, you are conservative.
You fight your conservatism with a fire that nearly destroys you.
You develop a charm that propels you.

I'm not gonna be able to [. . .] you can fill in the blank.
Sooorrrrry!

Oooh, I'm such a bad boy. Come suck my dick, sweetie. Aaah.

I do love you
Totally
Completely
Ridiculously
Hopelessly

Hunh?

3

WHY NOT YOU?

We would need to learn each other's languages
before we could understand what the other is babbling about.

You can't expect me to be as complexly perverted as that.

What?

I said as complexitivity perverdant aftershave fingerspring.

Who is willing to put up with how much in exchange for what?

Love and friendship—something like that.

Lovers dance the
Give-and-Take Tango.

Hey, could somebody turn the music up?

4

How DO YOU get up in the morning and go about the business of living?

Aggressive submission

Submissive aggression

Nordic sex

Sick sex

Trick codex

Public simplex

Bootlick sex

It's over. Terribly over. You're not worth fighting for, I keep telling myself, when all I want is you.

Give me the big-band tradition.

How do you forget about the self?

5

". . . AND IF THERE IS no self then whose arthritis is this?"

It should really be called selves. There are so many of us
assembled here.

Emotion is a sensualistic manifestation of life.

On how life is: I try.

How much can you obsess about a boy?

6

YOU DIG?
sick gooey obsession oozing
getting worse by the minute
paranoid fantasies out of control
like some cheap Hollywood version

Settle the mind.
Settle the mind.

Être nourit chez Nurit: Tansman again. Sans toi, naturellement.
And I agree with your tacit proposal to break here.

But it's a bloodbath.

The great surgery is underway and the patient is bleeding
profusely.
I've seen this done before and it wasn't pretty.

Did our love making not please?

7

How many hints before I take one?
I finally got it. It's clear now it's over.
Love has given me wings. They are damaged, but I think
I can still fly.

(Away from you.)

Letting someone down easy can't be easy.

On what terms am I the person I am?

8

CAN LONELINESS KILL?

You read about certain female characters in Victorian novels who are seen wandering the streets alone, alienated, and half mad. They end badly and die of malnutrition or suicide, or if they are better moneyed, they turn into grotesque old figures who frighten children.

Come back to your breath—notice it, draw it, and there you have your refuge.

What is real?

9

WHAT HAPPENS WHEN you lose control over your thoughts?

A new direction must be taken.

Yes, you caught me in the middle of grieving.
The sadness must be palpable and the smell of death, abhorrent.

How much pain am I willing to take on here?

10

Is LILLY LILLY Lilly Lilly Stay! addressed to a dog?

Titles for Montgomery Smith's sculptures:

NANCY PARKED HER CAR

STAY LILLY STAY

OH SHWEETIE

I DIDN' WANT YOU IN MY LIFE

GRUNT ALL YOU WANT

INTENSELY INVOLVED

IN THE BLINK OF AN EYE

CHASING SLEEP

PENELOPE HAS A GOAT

I'M A COMPLETE FAILURE

BLUES IN THE NIGHT

GUS [FOR THE SATYR]

Where to from here?

11

WHY DOES EVERY man I see remind me of wanting *you*?
It's an attraction I can't explain.

You see my poverty, my age, and you withdraw as if to keep from
catching a disease. When I contact you, you are indignant.

Who am I dealing with here? An insane member of the
community?
Someone who needs care? Am I insane too?

Is the idea to ride people, and hound them until they turn against
you and then you can feel wronged?

12

Is it evil just to be alive?
Having to fight is horrible. Monstrous.
I am shocked at the state of things.
I can barely participate enough to save my life.
I want out, but can't.
There really is No Exit.

You are monstrous in your horrid behavior.

I never thought I'd fall for someone like you.

Quick, how do we disentangle?

13

HOW CAN THERE be truth in an ever changing universe?
mitgefuehl
I beg your pardon?
I said *mitgefuehl*, which is German for compassion.
And why bring up compassion when we talk about truth in a
changing universe?
Because I seem to have lost my sense of humor.

Staring at the sunlit grass reminds me of childhood.
Grass-staring was a big thing back then. I remember this.

How can there be a universe in an ever changing truth?

14

NIRVANA ?

No more surgeries. I've just decided. If there is bad news (a recurrence) they will be met with different solutions. Yeah, you always say that, but when the time comes you try everything.

Being, these days, means being alone
Seeing others taking their turn at being happy
Feeling blue

WHATS THE MATTER DONT YOU LIKE IT HERE

15

DEATH IS SO incremental that we hardly notice that it's the same as life. The wheels are already in motion.

Not much depth to that boy, that's the trouble. Don't know why I should be so taken by him. There is a strong life force there, but he wants to be in control of what happens, so much so, that nothing much can really happen.

He is a strangler.

In his spare time he does axe murdering.

And the question is what do you want with a guy like that?

16

I FELL IN love with the idea of falling in love, not with you.
There.
Is this believable? To anyone but me.

You have your life and are following the plan. Your
responsibilities you want to live up to. Totally laudable. But there
is some acting out toward me, who did nothing to you, other
than suddenly appear in your life. I can just as suddenly
disappear—as I must.

Ask me a question.

17

SOME QUESTIONS CANNOT be asked, let alone answered.

Definitely.

                    Silence.

                                      Omen.

       Basement.

                                        Secret.

                Darker.

                    Deeper.

I know who you are: You are divine and precious
but something's wrong with you.
And it's not what you think.
It has to do with integrity.

Did she really? Mrs. Ginsberg on the 4th floor?

18

Does the elephant in the room ever say anything?
Anything sensible, I mean?

We're dealing here with an inexplicable preoccupation.

Some deaths are slow and measured. We don't dissolve so easily.
We know that *ars longa, vita brevis est.*

We are well, insofar as we are at all.
Buried in our work, not the cemetery.

Thank you for the relentless fight for human rights.
Your entire life.

No question.

19

SPIRIT CRUISES?

I'm stuck on you. Uplifted and dropped, as if by a
faulty mechanism.

I'll pick the trash. I'll live in the ruin. I'll take the leftovers.

Now that you have shown your icy heart, I want you even more.

An aberration. What's aberrant is the action's negation contained
within itself.

So yes: No expectations, not even justified ones, especially not
those. These are your rules.

Wounded pride and misplaced dignity.

I, too, had to harden my heart to survive.

This is how I come: I melt into a pool of intense pleasure. As
strong as a clitoral one, lasting about as long, not as sharp. Who
knows what's going on here. With you, nothing counts. To you,
everything is equally (un)important. Lately, you've opted for
sickness.
I'd say, be careful.

(no question)

20

I'M SO LONELY it hurts. A sweet, but searing, pain that makes
me hard to be with. Is that it? Maybe not at all.

There will be ten horses
Spirit Cruises
Gentle breezes
Warriors who think well of themselves
Killing machines and war profiteering
Misguided statesmen

Statespeople?

21

HAVE YOU NOTICED my eloquence?

My elegant software
My healing-plants

I can let go of my worries at the drop of a hat, the flip of a switch

I breathe and I listen to ambient sounds.

I observe the visual composition before me.

I am being mindful.

An apartment on Miami Beach. An amusing dream of turquoise
palm trees, heated pools, and pink lights. Or was that in L.A.? I
forget.

Man, you've been places! You better believe it sonny
(cackle cackle). I've been around the edge a few times.

And found that much is about restraint and mindfulness.
Courtesy, empathy, focus.

Doesn't that sound exactly right?

22

SHALL IPOD WHILE YouTube?

I am new today
I was new yesterday
I may be new tomorrow
But "the future is now."

Funk and brillo maturation
Allusion fenestration
Maggie's Paratransit
Quagmire zoloft antithesis

Where does all this skittishness come from?

23

CAN AN ORGANISM and its psyche be both delicate and resilient
at the same time?

To lift to say to brag to beg to hear to sweep

To repel to detest to replace to resent

Not to give in—not to succumb

Not to wallow not to slouch

Not to slip not to fall

To live to do to give to love

If I'm not well off does that mean I'm well on?

24

Is TENDERNESS a form of vulnerability?

Amiability instant hypoglycemic vis à vis the parlor pallor's
affability.

Parlor pallor.

Seemingly senselessly divided into "impossible-to-love" and
"must-love" groups
From which to choose requires tact.

Don't, do not, *ne pas*, show your naked insides to anyone
Your smelly intimate thoughts
Save them for later
Nobody profits from your excreta, except maybe you.
Yes, definitely you.

How come I don't know anyone in this room?

25

MUSIC WITH BRAINS?
Listen to this!

We're all suddenly silent
Gerrimander flabbergast

Even when we're together
Antifreeze kneecap
Humble demolition

Externalizing angelic remorse
Nonsense veritas
Tuba

Is there anything cats like better than a
horizontally positioned human?

26

WHAT IS THIS vast otherness that surrounds us?

Abernathy fungibility
Singularity handshake epilog

Because he fits, goddammit, because he fits!

Humor in music
Receding courtship

Ankle-deep in semantics
Festering servitude

Ageless extermination buggery
Flower bed
Low on the horizon
Dilly-dally
shilly-shally
web-mastering dance step

The piano as a source of joy? You bet.

27

WHY DOES LONELINESS always get worse at night?
It gets worse, but "a good day can sneak up on you as
unexpectedly as a bad one."

Concentrate condensate calibrate liberate
Sing a bellyful

I came across the verb "efforting" today

Two boys licking each other gently boyishly
Whereas the vocalist from Europe
Jumpy skittish brittle Europe
Pureope
Endureope
Sureope
Allureope
Manureope
Secureope
Insecureope
Captureope
Bravurope
Tenureope
Lureope
Tellyourope
Newrope

Modern man? Not anymore.

28

WHERE DID I put that toy fluid?

ovarian resolve

cabbage courage garbage
bamboo sandanista

the green flag
the great calm

getting here was hell
being here is hell
being here is not hell
getting here was not hell

I may need to dial it down a bit

But efforting?!

29

How should I know what's beautiful?

Let me know when it's happening.

"Thou shalt not" could be read as "It's not a good idea to"

take the advice without dropping to your knees
unless you feel the need to drop to them

Active participation

you create what you need
you cultivate the seeds and watch it all grow

And why is this newlywed crying to herself?

30

WHY DO REPULSION and attraction concur?

A multiplicity of creation.
It must be crowded for this to happen.

Self important, willful, and oppressive. Character flaws.
  (Claws)

The abandoned lover's burning desire burns my insides

One of us will try very hard to forget

not realizing that forgetting is resolving back into nothing.

Alarmed at the magnitude of events, he cuts his losses, bails out.
What's so special about that? Happens every day.

Better luck next time?

31

DO WOMEN ROUTINELY take the anger they feel for their father
out on guys?

The artist's idea wants out and escapes through some vent:
Pshhhh-fffff

You figure out what's "coming to you" and you take it.

Just don't reach for what you don't really want.

Forever forge forward

And know that the plot works against us

Why did you run away like that?

32

More titles for Montgomery Smith's sculptures?

THE BATTLE : A DEATH SENTENCE

CHANGE OR DIE

LET'S PLAY SPLIT PERSONALITY

SOMETIMES THINGS ARE EXACTLY AS THEY SEEM

ELABORATELY YOURS

TEMPORARILY ETERNAL

Am I supposed to be making it all up as I go?

33

CAN THE SIGNIFICANCE of words be more misleading than
    their sound?

Whatever the act, the confusion, the drama, may have been
I unexpectedly fell in love

Everything else may have been an elaborate hoax
A travesty, as you say
But love was never seriously considered

So this was a surprise

Or was it?

34

HOW CAN ANYBODY think another person's side irrelevant?

Many kinds of facts are necessary.

Does instinct deserve more authority than rationality?

Nietzsche called Descartes "superficial"
[for recognizing only the authority of reason]

Your statuesque coldness toward the heated folly of my emotions

As if I was poison

The letting go of the reins
The symbolism in art
A need that tries to satisfy itself

Frequent retrogression

Is obedience a herd instinct?

35

You want nothing to have happened?
Turn back the clock?

I'd say, turn it back to when we were happy
Not all the way back

Unreality
Imagined reality

System restore.

Dazzle them with my shine.
Razzmatazz.

Timid little animals?

36

THE DOGS OF China?
The rats of Manhattan?
The goats of Chile?
The elephants of Sri Lanka?

Look at those pigs' faces in those trucks.

We can see that the subject of the act is in the action
And that the act itself is exactly its own subject

Who knew?

37

WHAT SCARES ME the most?
This terrifying hunger

This monstrous need to satisfy (or resist) a craving

You don't know you can't know what lies ahead
You can't know what I feel for you

I'm doomed to desire you
What a predicament

How do I go about the business of getting over you?

38

AM I REALLY addicted to another human being?

Nothing I crave more than the patriarch's attention.

His hairiness
His warm brown skin
His voice

When the patriarch takes me into his arms I am
elaborately his.

Bach teaches rigorous discipline which he rewards
Cage teaches there is music everywhere and rewards that way

Why does animalistic fear excite sexually?

39

FEAR AS A turn-on?

Because the reptilian brain routinely mistakes fear for desire.

Your manufactured distance does nothing to abate what's
between us.

You may have miscalculated this one.
Or I may have.

Why are the weeks zooming by strangely?

40

MUST I BE brave and cunning and fierce and astute to survive?

I am tranquil
by nature
on the lazy side

The hardworking one, the one full of compassion and kindness,
the one full of love for humanity, the one to whom I owe my life
had a different temperament

we became allies and devoted friends

we fought a lot

at the end
I told him that I felt I owed him my very life
and he said
"I feel the exact same way about *you*."

Who is going to become of me now?

41

THAT'S ALWAYS THE question.
Who are we going to become of us?

Who haven't we been?

Who dare we not be?

The beloved's foot fetish
The beloved's body temperature
The beloved's near insanity

Am I ruled by chemistry?

42

Is THERE A problem here?

Other than reeling from life's blows, I mean.

I don't really see it.
Not other than.
Not two.

Fly with the flock for a while.

No commitments. I might fly off anytime, you know
Don't expect me to be here tomorrow

Let's not get too creepy.

Everything is being dealt an equally fatal blow

I will fly for a stretch
Over the river
Then I will rest my body on the shore
And wave to you from there

Do you swim?

43

A REDUCTIO AD absurdum of the good child?

A spidermonkey takes a sip from a lake
A photographer sees this and posts the photo on the Net
A woman sends the image to a man
Thinking he would enjoy seeing Narcissus in disguise kissing his
reflection

Or would he?

44

Is THE SWEET fable of life a variety of experiences?

Something solemn serious and tender

Being more or less divine

Frog prince no longer wishes to talk to me
I kissed a frog and he denied having become a prince
Maybe I'm not the princess I thought I was

The crisis seems to be over—for now

45

Is it a time of luxury when there is a luxury of time?

A bright scintillating serenity within.
A hidden penchant to happiness.

Well-adjusted
functioning
and a bit at sea, so I don't outsmart myself.

self-trickery has me on my toes.

You are a fantasy based on a real character, the canvas for my
paint.

My luminance.

This happiness we both mistook for a potential instead of the
real thing, is not something to belittle

Shall we aggrandize it then?

46

The illusion of accomplishment?

A chance to change

Vegan phone harangue
Manufacture villainy

The illusion of desire.

Something infinitely sinister going on over where you are.

Not you, you.

What am I saying?

47

Is the complexity a bit overwhelming?

I just want to sit near you.

I like it a little creepy.
I feel like a lost sheep.

Or a lobster.
A fisherman and his dog and a lobster.

The lobster is the loser.
The fisherman is looser.
The dog wins.

Innocent and earnest
The dog is vigilant dedicated unquestioning enthusiastic

Did dogs and humans really invent each other?

48

Do I REALLY miss you or am I out of my mind?

I miss you.
I'm out of my mind.

A slow and measured prelude can settle the mind.

It's like a chess game. Full of thought.

We move around in realms we don't even understand.
We sleepwalk.

I loved you.

Did you notice?

49

Vascillating between tears and happiness.

Back and forth.
Never-ending contradictions within a narrow band
The part that's visible

Some of us turn their ardor into fanaticism

Some of us avert their eyes when they see ardor

They don't feel entitled
Yet they feel above it all

Trouble is always always always due to
a lack of understanding

Non- or miscommunication

Les boulevards de Paris
La Place St. Michel

L'automne

La nostalgie europeenne
L'europe nostalgique?

L'AUTOMNE ?

I expect a little degeneration
It's inevitable
Descending from a long line of having been around
Surviving
"Oh, you'll be alright: you're a survivor"

Fuck you
fuck you
and
fuck you!

What better punishment?

Printed in the United Kingdom
by Lightning Source UK Ltd.
132526UK00001B/226-231/P